The Gentleman's Fancy Block
A Classic For Today's Quilts
Building Blocks Series 1 — Book 6

Special thanks to the following
for the beautiful fabrics used
in the quilts in this book:

Exclusively Quilters

Henry Glass & Co.

Northcott

P&B Textiles

Paintbrush Studio

All quilt designs by Sandy Boobar and
Sue Harvey of Pine Tree Country Quilts,
www.pinetreecountryquilts.com.

Published by

All American Crafts, Inc.
7 Waterloo Road
Stanhope, NJ 07874
www.allamericancrafts.com

Publisher | **Jerry Cohen**

Chief Executive Officer | **Darren Cohen**

Product Development
Director | **Brett Cohen**

Editor | **Sue Harvey**

Proofreader | **Natalie Rhinesmith**

Art Director | **Kelly Albertson**

Illustrations | **Kathleen Geary, Roni Palmisano
& Chrissy Scholz**

Product Development
Manager | **Pamela Mostek**

Vice President/Quilting Advertising
& Marketing | **Carol Newman**

Printed in China
ISBN: 978-1-936708-02-4
UPC: 793573035257

www.allamericancrafts.com

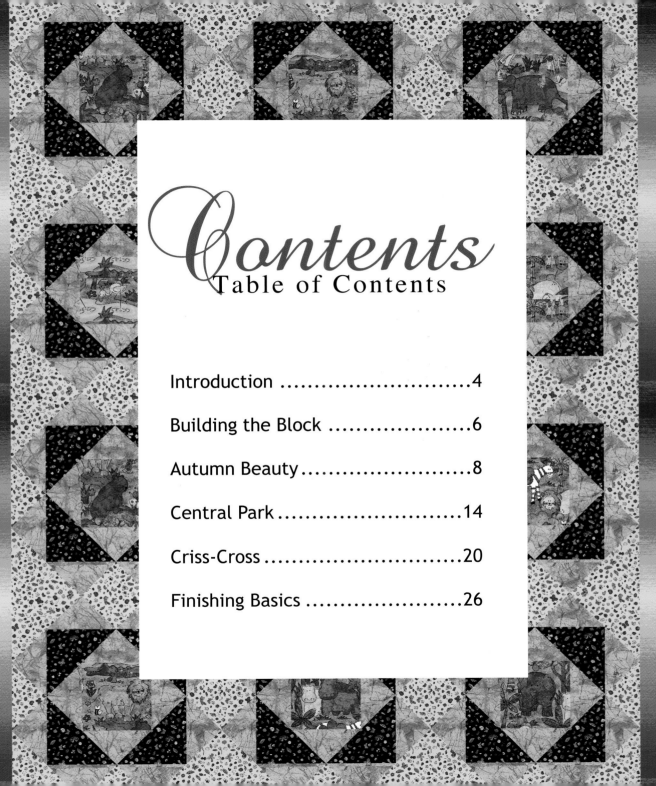

Contents
Table of Contents

Welcome to the Building Blocks series of quilting books.

Whether you're making your first or your one hundred and first quilt, the eight books in this series will be an invaluable addition to your quilting library. Besides featuring the instructions to make a different traditional and timeless block in each book, we've also included charts to give you all the quick information you need to change the block size for your own project.

Each book features complete instructions for three different quilts using the featured block with variations in size, color, and style—all designed to inspire you to use these timeless blocks for quilts with today's look.

The Finishing Basics section in each book gives you the tips and techniques you'll need to border, quilt, and bind the quilts in this book (or any quilt you may choose to make). If you're an experienced quilter, these books will be an excellent addition to your reference library. When you want to enlarge or reduce a block, the numbers are already there for you! No math required!

The blocks in the Building Blocks series of books have stood the test of time and are still favorites with quilters today. Although they're traditional blocks, they look very contemporary in today's bold and beautiful fabrics. This definitely puts them in the category of quilting classics!

For each block, you'll find a little background about its name, origin, or era, just to add a touch of quilting trivia. The block presented in this book is Gentleman's Fancy. Quilt historian Barbara Brackman found its first appearance in an 1894 periodical called the *Ohio Farmer*. It had no name. It was given its current name in 1922 by the Ladies Art Company in the mail-order catalog, *Quilt Patterns: Patchwork and Appliqué*.

In its early years, this block was usually made with only two fabrics—a light and a dark. The light was most often solid white, and, because it was so popular during the late 1800s, the dark was often indigo blue or red in small prints or solids. When the block was reintroduced as Gentleman's Fancy, it became popular in the fabrics of the time. Feed sacks and pastel colors made a big change in its look, with several colors of little prints or solids combined with white in a single block. The rounds of triangles glowed in bubblegum pink, delft blue, and sea green.

1890s

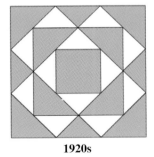
1920s

The quilts in this book take the Gentleman's Fancy block out of the light-dark theme. The rounds of triangles include lights, mediums, and darks in big prints, small prints, stripes, plaids, and polka dots. This block handles them all with ease and then springs a little surprise—a great secondary design forms when the blocks are joined in the quilt. Make your own surprise ending with your colors, your fabrics, your style!

Gentleman's Fancy

Use these instructions to make the blocks for the quilts in this book. The materials needed for each quilt and the cutting instructions are given with the pattern for the quilt. Also included is a Build It Your Way chart with a four different sizes for this block and the sizes to cut the pieces for one block. Use this information to design your own quilt or to change the size of any of the quilts in this book.

BUILDING THE BLOCK
Use a 1/4" seam allowance throughout.

1. Sew a B triangle to opposite sides of the A square. Press seams toward the B triangles. Sew a B triangle to the two remaining sides of the A square. Press seams toward the B triangles.

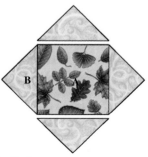

2. Stitch a C triangle to opposite sides of the pieced unit. Press seams toward the C triangles. Sew a C triangle to the two remaining sides of the pieced unit. Press seams toward the C triangles.

3. Sew a D triangle to each short side of an E triangle to make a DE strip. Press seams toward the E triangle. Repeat to make four DE strips total.

Make 4

4. Sew a DE strip to each side of the pieced unit. Press seams toward the pieced unit.

5. Sew an F triangle to each angled D edge of the pieced unit to complete the Gentleman's Fancy block. Press seams toward the F triangles.

6. Repeat to complete the number of blocks needed for the quilt that you have chosen.

Build It Better

Having trouble aligning the triangles with the squares? Fold the square in half and finger-press to make a crease. Align the corner of the triangle with the crease. The two sharp corners of the triangle should extend equally beyond the edges of the square.

Build It Better

Trim off those dog ears to reduce bulk before moving on to the next sewing step.

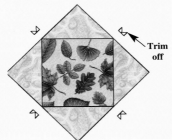

Trim off

Build It Your Way

Piece	9" Block	12" Block	15" Block	18" Block
A	$3\frac{1}{2}$" x $3\frac{1}{2}$"	$4\frac{1}{2}$" x $4\frac{1}{2}$"	$5\frac{1}{2}$" x $5\frac{1}{2}$"	$6\frac{1}{2}$" x $6\frac{1}{2}$"
B*	3" x 3"	$3\frac{3}{4}$" x $3\frac{3}{4}$"	$4\frac{3}{8}$" x $4\frac{3}{8}$"	$5\frac{1}{8}$" x $5\frac{1}{8}$"
C*	$3\frac{7}{8}$" x $3\frac{7}{8}$"	$4\frac{7}{8}$" x $4\frac{7}{8}$"	$5\frac{7}{8}$" x $5\frac{7}{8}$"	$6\frac{7}{8}$" x $6\frac{7}{8}$"
D**	$4\frac{1}{4}$" x $4\frac{1}{4}$"	$5\frac{1}{4}$" x $5\frac{1}{4}$"	$6\frac{1}{4}$" x $6\frac{1}{4}$"	$7\frac{1}{4}$" x $7\frac{1}{4}$"
E**	$4\frac{1}{4}$" x $4\frac{1}{4}$"	$5\frac{1}{4}$" x $5\frac{1}{4}$"	$6\frac{1}{4}$" x $6\frac{1}{4}$"	$7\frac{1}{4}$" x $7\frac{1}{4}$"
F*	$3\frac{7}{8}$" x $3\frac{7}{8}$"	$4\frac{7}{8}$" x $4\frac{7}{8}$"	$5\frac{7}{8}$" x $5\frac{7}{8}$"	$6\frac{7}{8}$" x $6\frac{7}{8}$"

Cut in half diagonally to make 2 triangles per square
**Cut twice diagonally to make 4 triangles per square*

Autumn Beauty

Don't want to deal with matching angled seams from block to block? Just add sashing! It also makes a great frame for the appliquéd setting blocks and, in a diagonal set, adds size to boost a quilt up to bed size.

Finished Quilt Size: 92½" x 92½"
Finished Block Size: 12" x 12"
Number of Blocks: 25
Skill Level: Confident Beginner

MATERIALS
All yardages are based on 42"-wide fabric.

- ½ yard of leaf print
- 2⅓ yards of cream print
- 2½ yards of rust texture
- 2⅜ yards of green texture
- 3 yards of brown paisley
- 8⅝ yards of backing fabric
- 101" x 101" piece of batting
- Thread to match fabrics
- 1¼ yards of 18"-wide fusible web (optional)
- Rotary cutting tools
- Basic sewing supplies

CUTTING

Label all pieces with the letters assigned. They will be used throughout the instructions.

From the leaf print, cut
- 3 strips 4 1/2" x 42"; recut into (20) 4 1/2" A squares

From the cream print, cut
- 4 strips 3 3/4" x 42"; recut into (40) 3 3/4" squares, then cut each square in half diagonally to make 80 B triangles
- 2 strips 12 1/2" x 42"; recut into (5) 12 1/2" G squares
- 2 strips 18 1/4" x 42"; recut into (3) 18 1/4" K squares and (2) 9 3/8" L squares, then cut the K squares twice diagonally to make 12 K triangles and the L squares in half diagonally to make 4 L triangles

From the rust texture, cut
- 5 strips 4 7/8" x 42"; recut into (40) 4 7/8" squares, then cut each square in half diagonally to make 80 C triangles
- 22 strips 2" x 42"; recut into (64) 2" x 12 1/2" H strips

From the green texture, cut
- 5 strips 5 1/4" x 42"; recut into (40) 5 1/4" squares, then cut each square twice diagonally to make 160 D triangles
- 2 strips 2" x 42"; recut into (24) 2" I squares
- 1 strip 3 3/8" x 42"; recut into (4) 3 3/8" squares, then cut each square twice diagonally to make 16 J triangles
- 8 strips 2 1/2" x 42" for inner border
- 10 strips 2 1/4" x 42" for binding

From the brown paisley, cut
- 3 strips 5 1/4" x 42"; recut into (20) 5 1/4" squares, then cut each square twice diagonally to make 80 E triangles
- 5 strips 4 7/8" x 42"; recut into (40) 4 7/8" squares, then cut each square in half diagonally to make 80 F triangles
- 9 strips 6 1/2" x 42" for outer border

From the backing fabric, cut
- 3 pieces 101" long

MAKING THE GENTLEMAN'S FANCY BLOCKS

Use a 1/4" seam allowance throughout unless otherwise instructed.

1. Refer to Building the Block on page 6 to make (20) 12 1/2" x 12 1/2" Gentleman's Fancy blocks.

Make 20

MAKING THE LEAF BLOCKS

1. For fusible appliqué, trace 20 leaf shapes onto the paper side of the fusible web, using the full-size pattern given on page 12.

2. Cut out each leaf, leaving a margin around the outside of the marked line.

3. Fuse to the wrong side of the rust texture.

4. Cut out each leaf on the marked line. Remove the paper backing. Continue with step 9.

5. For turned-edge appliqué, make a template for the leaf, using the full-size pattern given on page 12.

6. Trace 20 leaf shapes onto the right side of the rust tonal.

7. Cut out each leaf, adding a 1/4" seam allowance all around.

8. Turn the edges of each leaf under to the marked line. Press.

9. Fold the cream G squares twice diagonally and finger-press to mark the diagonal centers.

10. Place a leaf 3" from each corner on the creased diagonal lines.

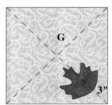 
Make 5

11. For fusible appliqué, fuse the leaves in place following the manufacturer's instructions for the fusible web. Machine-stitch around the outside edge of each leaf using matching or contrasting thread and the stitch of choice.

12. For turned-edge appliqué, pin the leaves in place. Hand- or machine-stitch the outside edge of each leaf to the G background squares.

Build It Better

Reduce the stiffness of fusible web! Trace the leaf onto the paper side of the fusible web. Cut out the center of the leaf, leaving 1/2" inside the marked line. Follow the instructions for fusible appliqué in Making the Leaf Blocks. When complete, the leaf will have fusible web around the outside edges only.

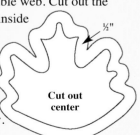
1/2"
Cut out center

COMPLETING THE QUILT TOP

1. Join the blocks and cream K triangles with rust H strips in seven diagonal rows. Press seams toward the H strips.

Make 2

Make 2

Make 2

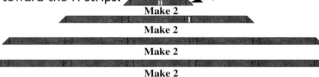
Make 1

2. Join rust H strips, green I squares, and green J triangles to make eight sashing rows. Press seams toward the H strips.

Make 2

Make 2

Make 2

Make 2

3. Join the block rows with the sashing rows and add a cream L triangle to each angled corner to complete the 77" x 77" quilt center. Press seams toward the sashing rows and L triangles. (Refer to the Quilt Assembly Diagram on page 12.)

4. Sew the 2 1/2" x 42" green texture strips short ends together to make a long strip. Press seams in one direction. Cut into two 77" strips and two 81" strips. Sew the shorter strips to opposite sides and the longer strips to the remaining sides of the quilt center. Press seams toward the strips. *Note: Refer to Finishing Basics on page 26 for information about cutting border strips.*

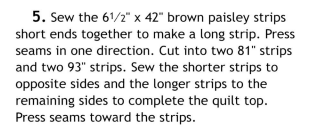

5. Sew the 6 1/2" x 42" brown paisley strips short ends together to make a long strip. Press seams in one direction. Cut into two 81" strips and two 93" strips. Sew the shorter strips to opposite sides and the longer strips to the remaining sides to complete the quilt top. Press seams toward the strips.

FINISHING THE QUILT

1. Remove the selvage edges from the backing pieces. Sew the pieces together down the length with a 1/2" seam allowance. Trim the sides to make a 101" x 101" backing piece. Press seams open.

2. Refer to Finishing Basics to layer, quilt, and bind your quilt.

Quilt Assembly Diagram

Full-size leaf pattern

12

Substitute a print for the setting squares and forget about the appliqué!
Contemporary garden prints make this version of *Autumn Beauty* light and lively.

Central Park

This basic setting for the Gentleman's Fancy blocks goes together like taking a stroll through the park—nice and easy, with lots of amazing things to discover. There are so many possibilities for making really creative secondary designs as the pieces from block to block meet. This is one of those designs that just demands colored pencils and graph paper. So sit down and start coloring!

Finished Quilt Size: 58" x 73"
Finished Block Size: 15" x 15"
Number of Blocks: 12
Skill Level: Confident Beginner/Intermediate

MATERIALS
All yardages are based on 42"-wide fabric.

❖ $5/8$ yard of brown floral
❖ $1/2$ yard of white floral
❖ $7/8$ yard of green print
❖ $7/8$ yard of white print
❖ $2 1/4$ yards of green floral
❖ 1 yard of brown print
❖ $4 5/8$ yards of backing fabric
❖ 66" x 81" piece of batting
❖ Thread to match fabrics
❖ Rotary cutting tools
❖ Basic sewing supplies

CUTTING

Label all pieces with the letters assigned. They will be used throughout the instructions.

From the brown floral, cut
- 3 strips $5^1/2$" x 42"; recut into (16) $5^1/2$" A squares

From the white floral, cut
- 3 strips $4^3/8$" x 42"; recut into (24) $4^3/8$" squares, then cut each square in half diagonally to make 48 B triangles

From the green print, cut
- 4 strips $5^7/8$" x 42"; recut into (24) $5^7/8$" squares, then cut each square in half diagonally to make 48 C triangles

From the white print, cut
- 4 strips $6^1/4$" x 42"; recut into (24) $6^1/4$" squares, then cut each square twice diagonally to make 96 D triangles

From the green floral, cut
- 2 strips $6^1/4$" x 42"; recut into (12) $6^1/4$" squares, then cut each square twice diagonally to make 48 E triangles
- 4 strips $5^7/8$" x 42"; recut into (24) $5^7/8$" squares, then cut each square in half diagonally to make 48 F triangles
- 6 strips $5^1/2$" x 42" for outer border

From the brown print, cut
- 6 strips 2" x 42" for inner border
- 7 strips $2^1/4$" x 42" for binding

From the backing fabric, cut
- 2 pieces 81" long

MAKING THE GENTLEMAN'S FANCY BLOCKS

Use a $1/4$" seam allowance throughout unless otherwise instructed.

1. Refer to Building the Block on page 6 to make (12) $15^1/2$" x $15^1/2$" Gentleman's Fancy blocks.

Make 12

COMPLETING THE QUILT TOP

1. Sew three blocks together to make a row. Press seams in one direction. Repeat to make four rows total.

Make 4

2. Join the rows to complete the 45$\frac{1}{2}$" x 60$\frac{1}{2}$" quilt center. Press seams in one direction. (Refer to the Quilt Assembly Diagram on page 18.)

3. Sew the 2" x 42" brown print strips short ends together to make a long strip. Press seams in one direction. Cut into two 60$\frac{1}{2}$" strips and two 48$\frac{1}{2}$" strips. Sew the longer strips to the long sides and the shorter strips to the top and bottom of the quilt center. Press seams toward the strips. ***Note: Refer to Finishing Basics on page 26 for information about cutting border strips.***

4. Stitch the 5$\frac{1}{2}$" x 42" green floral strips short ends together to make a long strip. Press seams in one direction. Cut into two 63$\frac{1}{2}$" strips and two 48$\frac{1}{2}$" strips. Sew the longer strips to the long sides of the quilt center. Press seams toward the strips.

5. Sew a brown floral A square to each end of the 48$\frac{1}{2}$" green floral strips. Press seams toward the green floral strips. Sew the pieced strips to the top and bottom to complete the quilt top. Press seams toward the strips.

FINISHING THE QUILT

1. Remove the selvage edges from the backing pieces. Sew the pieces together down the length with a $\frac{1}{2}$" seam allowance. Trim the sides to make a 66" x 81" backing piece. Press seam open.

2. Refer to Finishing Basics to layer, quilt, and bind your quilt.

Build It Better

Having trouble matching the angled seams when joining the blocks in rows? Mark a line on the wrong side of a block $\frac{1}{4}$" from the edge across the angled seams. Place the marked block right sides together with another block. Fold the edge of the marked block back on the $\frac{1}{4}$" line. The angled seams should intersect with the seams of the second block. Adjust, if necessary. Pin the blocks at each seam to hold for stitching.

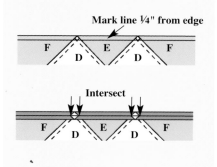

Build It Better

Make a sweet baby quilt—same fabrics, same pattern! Refer to the Build It Your Way chart on page 7 to make 9" blocks instead of the 15" blocks used in the lap-size quilt. Then cut the borders 1½" wide and 3½" wide to make a 35" x 44" quilt.

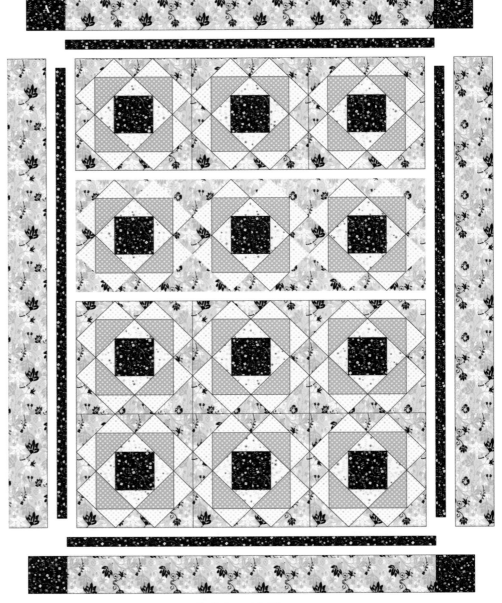

Quilt Assembly Diagram

Central Park becomes *Central Zoo* in this version of the quilt! Notice that the focus is on the yellow squares that form when the blocks are joined. They seem to be jumping right out of the quilt, while everything else settles into the background.

Criss-Cross

A simple pieced border adds lots of interest to the X design of this quilt. It makes the large setting triangles an important part of the quilt center—not just something to square out the edges.

Finished Quilt Size: 63" x 63"
Finished Block Size: 18" x 18"
Number of Blocks: 5
Skill Level: Confident Beginner

MATERIALS
All yardages are based on 42"-wide fabric.

❖ 1/3 yard of fireworks print
❖ 1/3 yard of red bandanna print
❖ 1 yard of cream star print
❖ 1 1/8 yards of red star print
❖ 1/2 yard of navy pin dot
❖ 5/8 yard of light blue floral
❖ 1 1/2 yards of medium blue floral
❖ 1 yard of cream floral
❖ 4 1/8 yards of backing fabric
❖ 71" x 71" piece of batting
❖ Thread to match fabrics
❖ Rotary cutting tools
❖ Basic sewing supplies

CUTTING

Label all pieces with the letters assigned. They will be used throughout the instructions. All pieces labeled with a letter and 1 are for the red blocks; those labeled with a letter and 2 are for the navy block.

From the fireworks print, cut
- 1 strip 6$\frac{1}{2}$" x 42"; recut into (4) 6$\frac{1}{2}$" A1 squares

From the red bandanna print, cut
- 1 strip 6$\frac{1}{2}$" x 42"; recut into (1) 6$\frac{1}{2}$" A2 square

From the cream star print, cut
- 2 strips 5$\frac{1}{8}$" x 42"; recut into (10) 5$\frac{1}{8}$" squares, then cut each square in half diagonally to make 20 B triangles
- 1 strip 5$\frac{1}{2}$" x 42"; recut into (5) 5$\frac{1}{2}$" I squares and (4) 3" K squares, then cut the I squares twice diagonally to make 20 I triangles and the K squares in half diagonally to make 8 K triangles
- 4 strips 2$\frac{5}{8}$" x 42"; recut into (4) 2$\frac{5}{8}$" x 13$\frac{1}{4}$" L strips and (4) 2$\frac{3}{8}$" x 15$\frac{3}{8}$" M strips

From the red star print, cut
- 2 strips 6$\frac{7}{8}$" x 42"; recut into (8) 6$\frac{7}{8}$" squares, then cut each square in half diagonally to make 16 C1 triangles
- 7 strips 2$\frac{1}{4}$" x 42" for binding

From the navy pin dot, cut
- 1 strip 6$\frac{7}{8}$" x 42"; recut into (2) 6$\frac{7}{8}$" squares, then cut each square in half diagonally to make 4 C2 triangles
- 1 strip 5$\frac{1}{2}$" x 42"; recut into (6) 5$\frac{1}{2}$" squares, then cut each square twice diagonally to make 24 J triangles

From the light blue floral, cut
- 2 strips 7$\frac{1}{4}$" x 42"; recut into (10) 7$\frac{1}{4}$" squares, then cut each square twice diagonally to make 40 D triangles

From the medium blue floral, cut
- 1 strip 7$\frac{1}{4}$" x 42"; recut into (5) 7$\frac{1}{4}$" squares, then cut each square twice diagonally to make 20 E triangles
- 2 strips 6$\frac{7}{8}$" x 42"; recut into (10) 6$\frac{7}{8}$" squares, then cut each square in half diagonally to make 20 F triangles
- 6 strips 4$\frac{1}{2}$" x 42" for outer border

From the cream floral, cut
- 1 strip 28" x 42"; recut into (1) 26$\frac{3}{4}$" G square and (2) 13$\frac{5}{8}$" H squares, then cut the G square twice diagonally to make 4 G triangles and the H squares in half diagonally to make 4 H triangles

From the backing fabric, cut
- 2 pieces 71" long

MAKING THE GENTLEMAN'S FANCY BLOCKS

Use a $\frac{1}{4}$" seam allowance throughout unless otherwise instructed.

1. Refer to Building the Block on page 6 to make four 18$\frac{1}{2}$" x 18$\frac{1}{2}$" red Gentleman's Fancy blocks, using A1, B, C1, D, E, and F pieces.

Make 4

Make 1

2. Refer to Building the Block on page 6 to make one 18½" x 18½" navy Gentleman's Fancy block, using A2, B, C2, D, E, and F pieces.

COMPLETING THE QUILT TOP

1. Sew a cream G triangle to opposite sides of a red block to make a diagonal corner row. Press seams toward the triangles. Repeat to make a second diagonal corner row.

Make 2

2. Stitch the navy block between two red blocks to make the diagonal center row. Press seams toward the navy block. *Note: Refer to Build It Better on page 17 for help in matching the angled seams of the blocks.*

Make 1

3. Sew the center row between the corner rows. Press seams toward the corner rows. Add a cream H triangle to each angled corner to complete the 51½" x 51½" quilt center. Press seams toward the triangles. (Refer to the Quilt Assembly Diagram on page 24.)

4. Sew six navy J triangles alternately together with five cream I triangles to make a strip. Press seams toward the navy triangles. Sew a cream K triangle to each end of the pieced strip. The strip should measure 2⅝" x 26". Repeat to make four pieced strips total.

Make 4

Build It Better

Use a scant ¼" seam allowance to join the triangles in the pieced border. It's easier to take a bit deeper seam if the strip is a little too long than to take out seams and restitch if the strip is a little too short.

5. Sew a cream L strip to each end of a pieced strip. Press seams toward the L strips. Repeat to make a second strip. Center and pin the strips to opposite sides of the quilt center. The navy triangle edge of the strips should fit along the edge of the large G triangle between the corners of the blocks. Sew the strips in place. Press seams toward the quilt center.

6. Sew a cream M strip to each end of the remaining pieced strips. Press seams toward the M strips. Center and pin the strips to the remaining sides of the quilt center. Sew the strips in place. Press seams toward the quilt center.

7. Sew the 4½" x 42" medium blue floral strips short ends together to make a long strip. Press seams in one direction. Cut into two 55¾" strips and two 63¾" strips. Sew the shorter strips to opposite sides and the longer strips to the remaining sides to complete the quilt top. Press seams toward the strips. *Note: Refer to Finishing Basics on page 26 for information about cutting border strips.*

FINISHING THE QUILT

1. Remove the selvage edges from the backing pieces. Sew the pieces together down the length with a 1/2" seam allowance. Trim the sides to make a 71" x 71" backing piece. Press seam open.

2. Refer to Finishing Basics to layer, quilt, and bind your quilt.

Build It Better

Lots of triangles mean lots of bias edges. Take control! Apply a heavy coat of spray starch and press dry before doing any sewing. Then be sure to press—not iron—seams with an up-down motion, not a back-and-forth motion.

Quilt Assembly Diagram

Big blocks make for quick, changeable decorating! Where the original quilt is playful and patriotic, perfect for a summer celebration, this version is calm and subdued. A beautiful accent for the back of a sofa or the center of a bed in late summer or early autumn.

Finishing Basics

ADDING BORDERS

Borders are an important part of your quilt. They add another design element, and act much like a picture frame to complement and support the center.

There are two basic types of borders—butted corners and mitered corners. Butted corners are the most common. For this technique, border strips are stitched to opposite sides of the quilt center, pressed, and then strips are sewn to the remaining sides. Mitered corners are often used to continue a pattern around the corners; for example, the stripe in a fabric or a pieced border design.

Butted corners   **Mitered corners**

Lengths are given for the borders in the individual quilt instructions. In most cases, fabric-width strips are joined to make a strip long enough to cut two side strips and top and bottom strips. Because of differences in piecing and pressing, your quilt center may differ slightly in size from the mathematically exact size used to determine the border lengths. Before cutting the strips for butted corners, refer to the instructions given here to measure for lengths to fit your quilt center. For mitered borders, extra length is already included in the sizes given in the instructions to make it easier to stitch the miters. It should be enough to allow for any overall size differences.

BUTTED CORNERS

1. Press the quilt center. Arrange it on a flat surface with the edges straight.

2. Fold the quilt in half lengthwise, matching edges and corners. Finger-press the center fold to make a crease. Unfold.

3. Measure along the center ceased line to determine the length of the quilt center.

 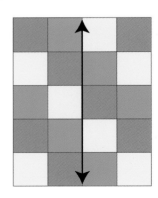

Fold in half

4. Cut two strips this length.

5. Fold the strips in half across the width and finger-press to make a crease.

6. Place a strip right sides together on one long edge of the quilt center, aligning the creased center of the strip with the center of the long edge. Pin in place at the center. Align the ends of the strips with the top and bottom edges of the quilt center. Pin in place at each end.

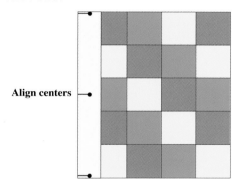

Align centers

7. Pin between the ends and center, easing any fullness, if necessary.

8. Stitch the border to the quilt center. Press.

9. Repeat on the remaining long edge.

10. Fold the quilt in half across the width and crease to mark the center. Unfold. Measure along the creased line to determine the width of the bordered quilt center.

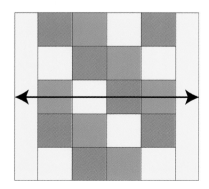

11. Cut two strips this length.

12. Repeat steps 5—9 on the top and bottom edges of the quilt center.

MITERED CORNERS

1. Prepare the border strips as directed in the individual pattern.

2. Make a mark 1/4" on each side of the quilt corners.

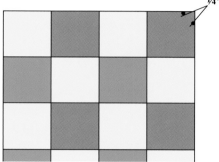

1/4"

3. Center the border strips on each side of the quilt top and pin in place. Stitch in place, stopping and locking stitches at the 1/4" mark at each corner.

4. Fold the quilt top in half diagonally with wrong sides together. Arrange two border ends right sides together.

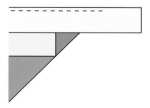

5. Mark a 45˚angle line from the locked stitching on the border to the outside edge of the border.

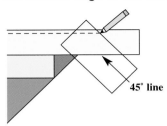

45° line

6. Stitch on the marked line, starting exactly at the locked stitch. Trim seam allowance to 1/4".

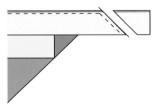

7. Press the mitered corner seam open and the seam between the border and the rest of the quilt toward the border.

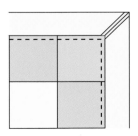

8. Repeat these steps on each corner of the quilt.

LAYERING, BASTING & QUILTING

You may choose to do your own quilting or take your projects to a machine quilter. Be sure that your backing and batting are at least 4" wider and 4" longer on each side of the quilt top. The size needed is given in the Materials list for each project.

If you would like to quilt your own project, there are many good books about hand and machine quilting. Check with your quilting friends or at your local quilt shop for recommendations. Here are the basic steps to do your own quilting:

1. Mark the quilt top with a quilting design, if desired.

2. Place the backing right side down on a flat surface. Place the batting on top. Center the quilt top right side up on top of the batting. Smooth all the layers. Thread-baste, pin, or spray-baste the layers together to hold while quilting.

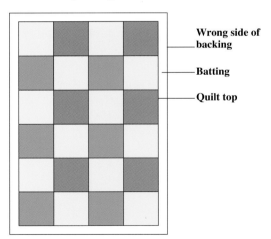

Wrong side of backing

Batting

Quilt top

3. Quilt the layers by hand or machine.

4. When quilting is finished, trim the batting and backing even with the quilted top.

BINDING

The patterns in this book include plenty of fabric to cut either 2¼" or 2½" wide strips for straight-grain, double-fold binding. In some cases, a wider binding or bias binding is needed because of a specific edge treatment; extra yardage is included when necessary.

PREPARING STRAIGHT-GRAIN, DOUBLE-FOLD BINDING

1. Cut strips as directed for the individual pattern. Remove selvage edges.

2. Place the ends of two binding strips right sides together at a right angle. Mark a line from inside corner to inside corner. Stitch on the marked line. Trim seam allowance to ¼".

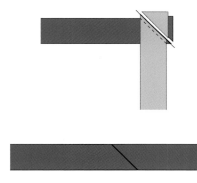

3. Repeat step 2 to join all binding strips into one long strip. Press seams to one side. Fold the strip in half lengthwise with wrong sides together and press.

PREPARING DOUBLE-FOLD BIAS BINDING

1. Cut an 18" x 42" strip from the binding fabric.

2. Place the 45° angle line of a rotary ruler on one edge of the strip. Trim off one corner of the strip.

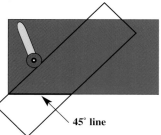

45° line

3. Cut binding strips in the width specified in the pattern from the angled end of the strip.

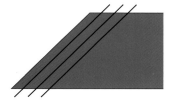

4. Each strip will be approximately 25" long. Cut strips to total the length needed for the pattern, repeating steps 1 and 2 if needed.

5. Align the ends of two strips with right sides together. Stitch ¼" from the ends.

6. Repeat to join all binding strips into one long strip. Press seams to one side.

ADDING THE BINDING

1. Leaving a 6"-8" tail and beginning several inches from a corner, align the raw edges of the binding with the edge of the quilt. Stitch along the edge with a 1/4" seam allowance, locking stitches at the beginning.

2. Stop 1/4" from the first corner and lock stitching. Remove the quilt from your machine. Turn the quilt so the next edge is to your right. Fold the binding end up and then back down so the fold is aligned with the previous edge of the quilt and the binding is aligned with the edge to your right. Starting at the edge of the quilt, stitch the binding to the next corner.

3. Repeat step 2 to attach binding to the rest of the quilt, stopping stitching 6"–8" from the starting point and locking stitches.

4. Unfold the ends of the strips. Press flat. About halfway between the stitched ends, fold the beginning strip up at a right angle. Press. Fold the ending strip down at a right angle, with the folded edge butted against the fold of the beginning end. Press.

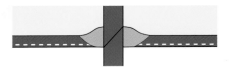

5. Trim each end 1/4" from creased fold. Place the trimmed ends right sides together. Pin to hold. Stitch 1/4" from the ends. Press the seam allowance open.

6. Refold the strip in half. Press. Arrange the strip on the edge of the quilt and stitch in place to finish the binding.

7. Fold the edge of the binding over the raw edges to the back of the quilt. Hand stitch in place, covering the machine stitches and mitering the corners.

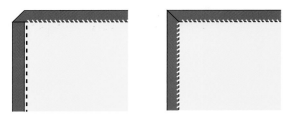

The **Dutchman's Puzzle** Block

Building Blocks Series 1 – Book 1

A Classic For Today's Quilts

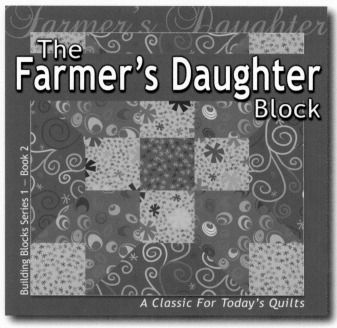

The **Farmer's Daughter** Block

Building Blocks Series 1 – Book 2

A Classic For Today's Quilts

The **Log Cabin** Block

Building Blocks Series 1 – Book 3

A Classic For Today's Quilts

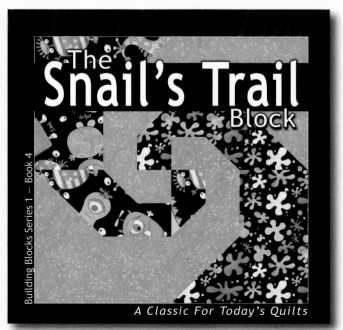

The **Snail's Trail** Block

Building Blocks Series 1 – Book 4

A Classic For Today's Quilts

Books 5-8 →

The Wild Goose Chase

Building Blocks Series 1 — Book 5

A Classic For Today's Quilts

The Gentleman's Fancy Block

A Classic For Today's Quilts

The Jacob's

Building Blocks Series 1 — Book 7

A Classic For Today's Quilts

tooth Star Block

Building Blocks S

A Classic For Today's Quilts

DISCARDED

DATE DUE

AUG 1 6 2012
OCT 1 3 2012

Demco, Inc. 38-293